DUDLEY
A Florida Manatee

by Bonnie Highsmith Taylor

Perfection Learning®

Cover Photo: Jeff Foott (www.jfoott.com)

Dedication
For Archie Griffin and Leon Griffin

About the Author
Bonnie Highsmith Taylor is a native Oregonian. She loves camping in the Oregon mountains and watching birds and other wildlife. Writing is Ms. Taylor's first love. But she also enjoys going to plays and concerts, collecting antique dolls, and listening to good music.

Image Credits
Jeff Foott (www.jfoott.com).

Text © 2000 Perfection Learning® Corporation.
All rights reserved. No part of this book may be used or reproduced in any manner whatsoever without written permission from the publisher.
Printed in the United States of America. For information, contact Perfection Learning® Corporation, 1000 North Second Avenue,
P.O. Box 500, Logan, Iowa 51546-0500.
Tel: 1-800-831-4190 • Fax: 1-800-543-2745
Paperback ISBN 0-7891-2841-1
Cover Craft® ISBN 0-7807-9000-6

3 4 5 6 7 PP 08 07 06 05 04

Contents

Chapter 1 6

Chapter 2 14

Chapter 3 24

Chapter 4 32

Chapter 5 39

Chapter 6 48

chapter 1

The manatee was ready to have her first calf. She had mated nearly 13 months ago.

Some animals mate only at certain times of the year. But manatees breed anytime.

Females are called cows. They weigh about 1,000 pounds. And they are up to ten feet long.

The water was shallow. The cow moved very slowly. Now and then, she felt a small pain. She gave a low squeak each time.

She was puzzled. She didn't know what was happening to her. She had never felt like this.

Once in a while, the cow stopped moving. She paused to eat some water hyacinth. She pushed the plant into her mouth with a flipper. She chewed slowly.

Manatees are herbivores. This means they only eat plants.

The cow felt a hard pain. It was harder than the others. She stopped chewing. She gave a low groan.

The cow rose to the top of the water. She needed air. Then back down she went.

Her pains lasted for two more hours. Finally, Dudley was born. He was born tail first.

The cow moved under her newborn calf. She lifted him to the top. He needed air right away.

Some scientists believe that baby manatees must learn to breathe. They think the calves don't know how at birth.

Dudley's mother kept him near the top. They stayed there a long time.

She nuzzled Dudley's face with her face. He put his mouth against hers. Nuzzling, or kissing, is a way of imprinting. Imprinting is a learning process. An animal learns to recognize its own kind.

Dudley would never forget his mother. And she, of course, wouldn't forget him.

Dudley weighed 64 pounds. He was nearly four feet long. That was from the tip of his muzzle, or nose, to the end of his fluke, or tail.

The cow raised a flipper. She had a nipple under each flipper. Dudley latched onto a nipple.

Dudley nursed underwater for a while. Then his mother brought him to the top to breathe.

Manatees must come up for air every three to five minutes. They must come up even when they sleep.

When they sleep or rest, their heartbeats slow down. Then they don't have to come up as often. They only breathe once about every 15 to 20 minutes.

They have small flaps of skin in their noses. The flaps open to let in air. They close to keep water out.

The water wasn't very deep where Dudley was born. Manatees like water that is less than eight or ten feet deep.

11

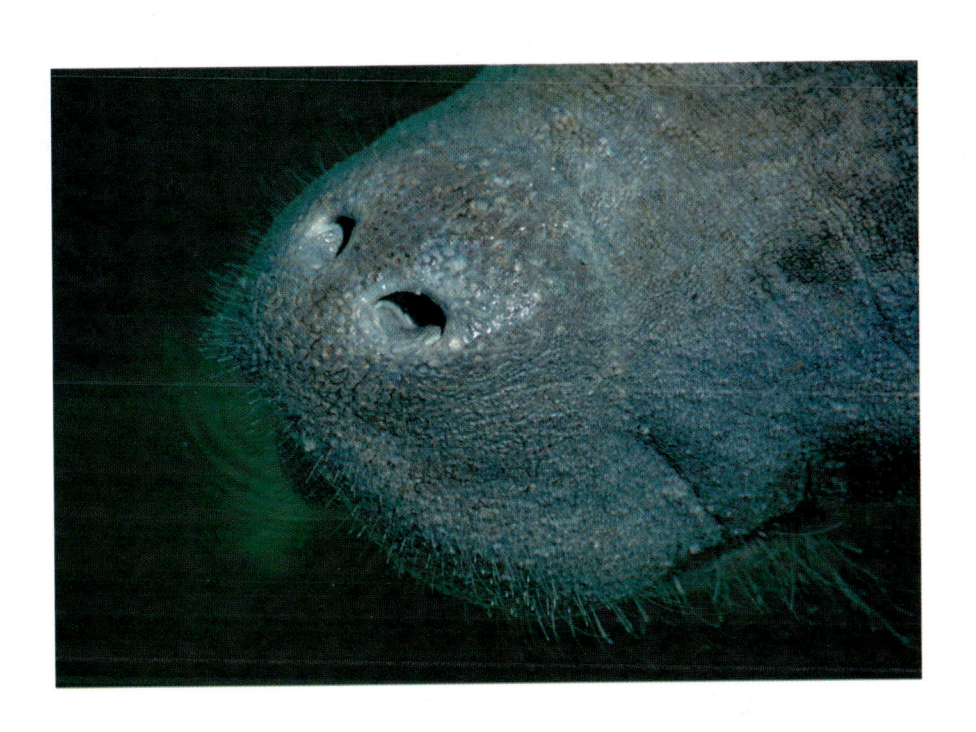

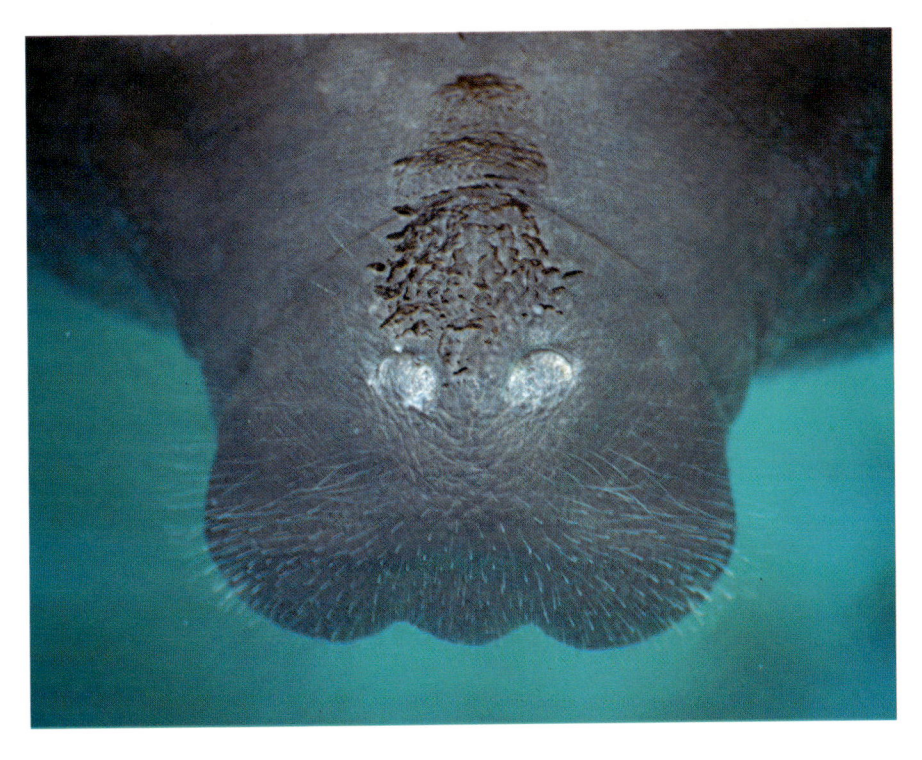

They can dive 25 feet. But they don't very often. Deep water is colder. And manatees need warm water.

Manatees get cold easily. They don't have much body fat. And fat acts like a blanket. It holds in body heat.

Dudley and his mother were West Indian

manatees. They were also called Florida manatees.

Florida manatees can live in saltwater or freshwater. But they seldom go far out to sea. They usually live in shallow, slow-moving rivers and bays. They also live in canals and coastal waters.

chapter 2

Dudley had just been born. And he had visitors already. Two cows and their calves came to see him.

The calves nuzzled Dudley. They wanted to play. But Dudley wasn't ready to play. He was getting used to living outside of his mother's body. He was still learning to breathe. And he was nursing.

Dudley wasn't afraid of the visitors. But he stayed close to his mother. His mother watched the visitors closely.

Manatees guard their young. The calves stay with their mothers for two years or more. They stay until the mother has another calf.

One of the cows nuzzled Dudley's mother. She nuzzled back.

One visitor had a large chunk of her tail missing. There were several other scars on her body. She had been hurt by a motorboat.

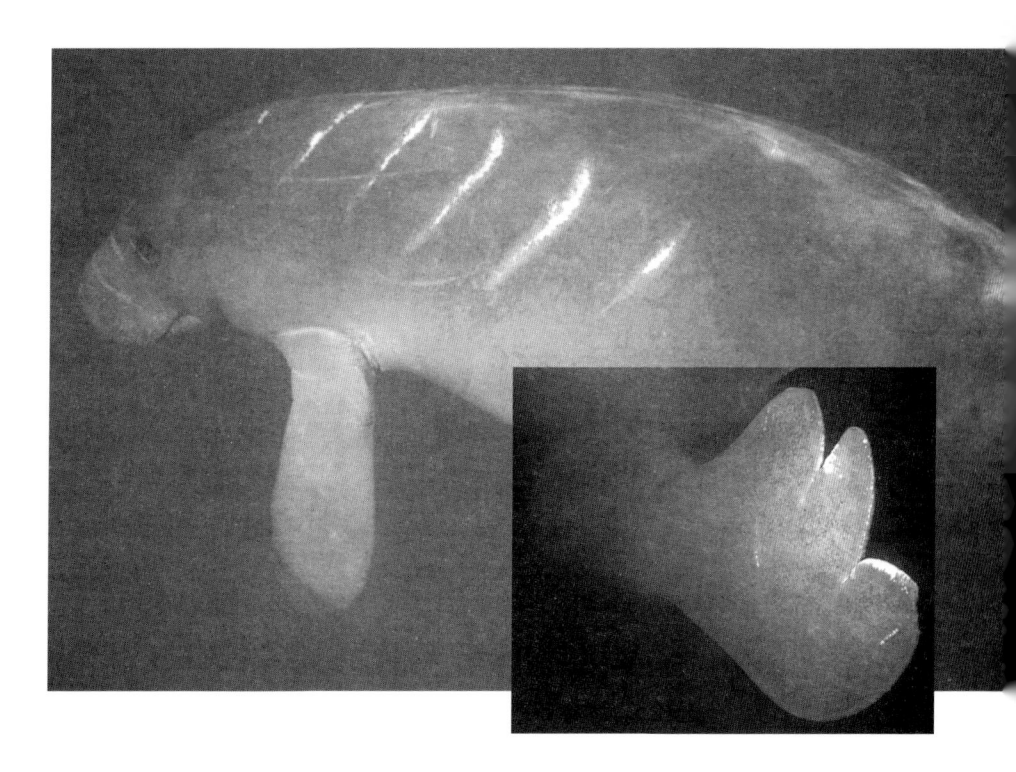

Manatees are often hit by boats. Sharp bottoms and propellers leave huge scars. Scientists recognize manatees by their scars.

Many manatees are killed by motorboats. The first reported death was in 1943.

In many waterways and narrow channels, there are speed limits for boats. But even so, many manatees are hurt or killed each year.

Others are crushed by floodgates. Some die from swallowing fishing hooks and lines. Some drown after being caught in fishing nets.

Manatees don't have natural predators. They die from human-related causes, natural causes, or diseases.

In 1996, close to 400 manatees died in Florida from red tide. Until then, there were about 2,400 manatees.

Red tide is a poison that comes from tiny living things. Manatees have been around red tide for years. It didn't seem to be harmful to them until now. Scientists believe that pollution has made red tide harmful.

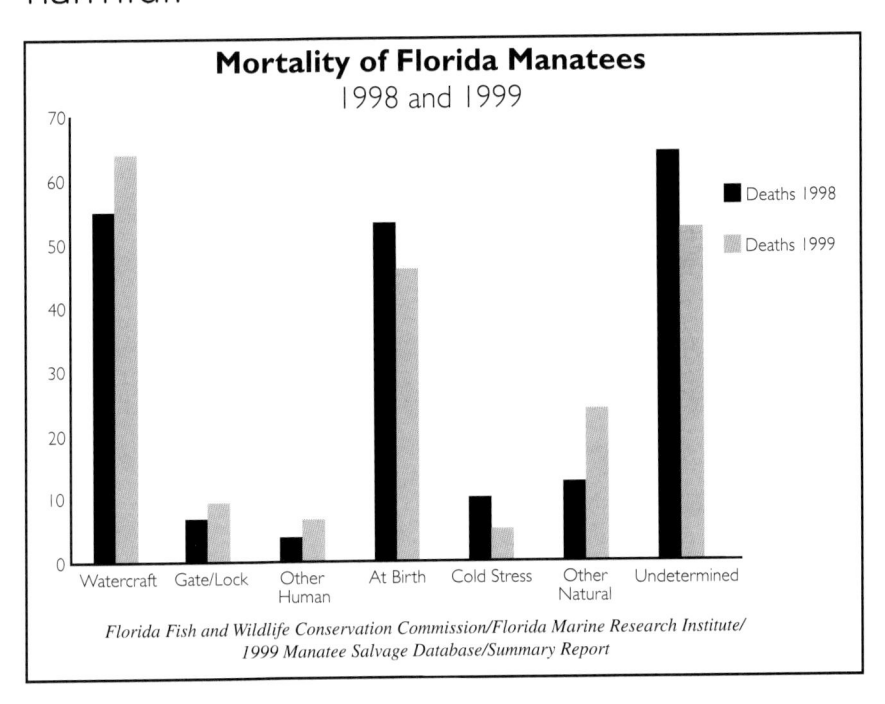

Mortality of Florida Manatees
1998 and 1999

Florida Fish and Wildlife Conservation Commission/Florida Marine Research Institute/ 1999 Manatee Salvage Database/Summary Report

After a while, Dudley's visitors left.

Dudley floated near the top. He stayed close to his mother. He nursed often. It would be several weeks before he would eat plants.

Like his mother, Dudley had very little hair. Manatees' body hair is thin. The hair around their mouths is very stiff. It's like a brush.

The manatee's upper lip is divided in half. It cuts and tears plants like pliers.

Several plants that manatees eat are very tough. Some animals would have trouble chewing them. But manatees don't. They have strong teeth.

Manatees don't have biting teeth. They only have teeth for chewing. These are called molars. They also have a hard, bony plate on the roof of their mouths.

There are about five or six molars in each part of their jaws. They chew a lot of sand and gravel with their food. So their teeth wear down fast.

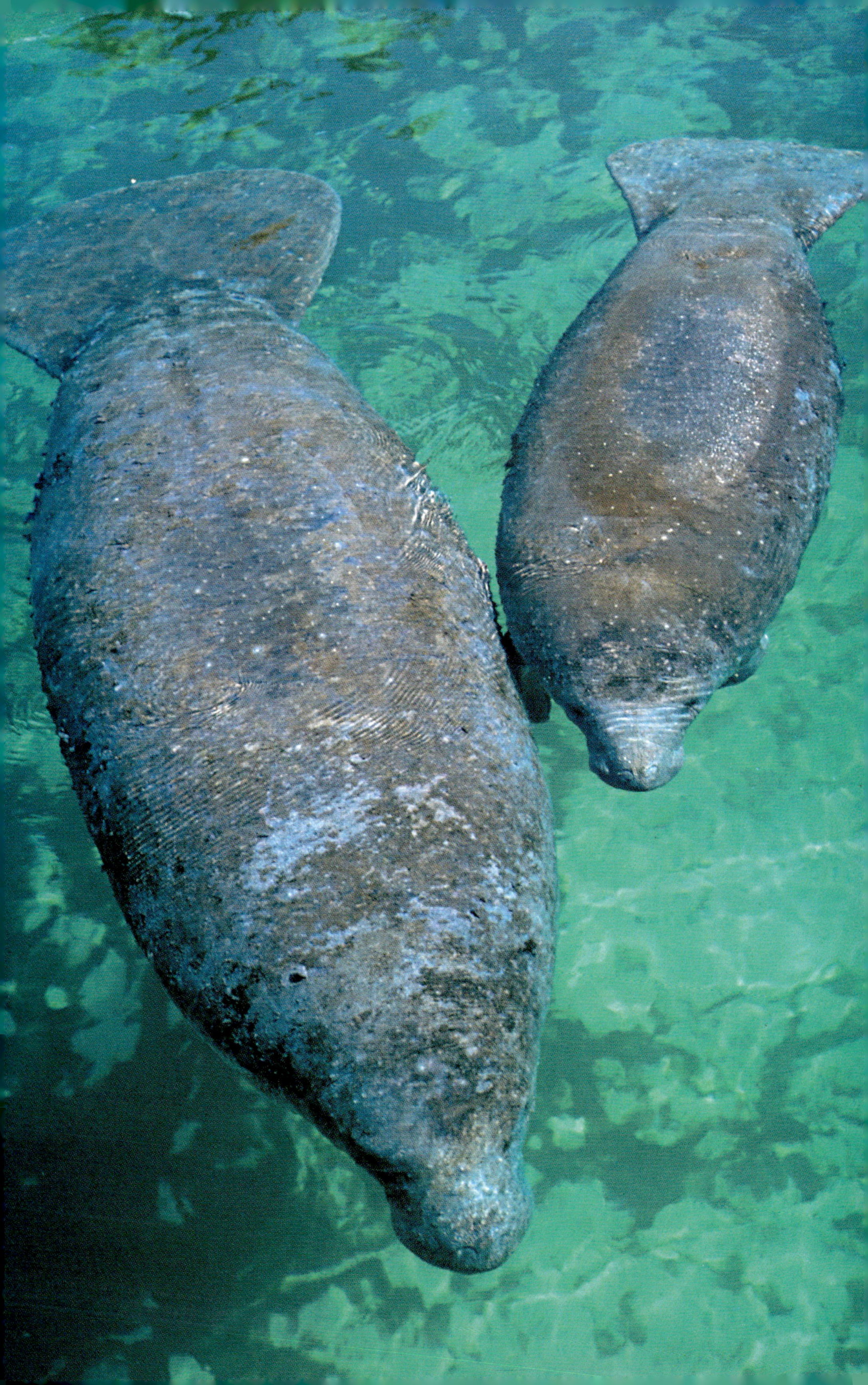

New molars grow all the time. As teeth wear down, new molars move forward. They push out the worn ones.

Manatees eat all kinds of grass—mainly ribbon, turtle, and manatee grass. They also eat hydrilla. This is a grassy plant that grows on the bottoms of rivers and streams.

There are some plants they won't eat. One is spatter dock. It tastes bitter.

Manatees prefer plants that grow on the river bottom. Their mouths seem suited for feeding on these.

Sometimes manatees crawl partway onto a bank to eat plants. They even eat acorns that fall into the water.

Manatees often dig up plants near the shore. The small fish scatter. So blue herons and other birds wait close by. Then it's easy for the birds to find fish to eat.

In captivity, manatees are fed lettuce, cabbage, carrots, and even hay.

Manatees chew their food well. On a quiet night, they can be heard chewing up to 200 yards away.

Dudley stayed close to his mother. When his mother swam around, he rode on her back.

He kept his tail tucked up close to his belly. He paddled with his flippers.

Adult manatees don't use their flippers for swimming. The adults swim by moving their flat, paddle-shaped tails up and down. But they move very slowly. They travel between two to four miles per hour.

This is one reason why so many are hurt by boats and jet skis. They can't get out of the way fast enough.

Adult manatees use their flippers to guide themselves as they swim. And they use them for pushing food into their mouths and for scratching themselves. They also use the flippers for cleaning their teeth.

23

chapter 3

Every day, Dudley grew bigger and stronger. Manatees grow very fast. They double their weight in about two months.

Dudley was like all calves. He loved to play.

He played with other calves. They chased each other. They dived to the bottom of the water. Then up they'd come. They bumped each other with their noses.

Sometimes there were no calves around. So Dudley played with his mother. He nibbled her playfully with his lips. She nibbled him back.

Dudley often found something floating on the water. He would push it all around with his nose. A piece of floating wood made a fine toy for the young calf.

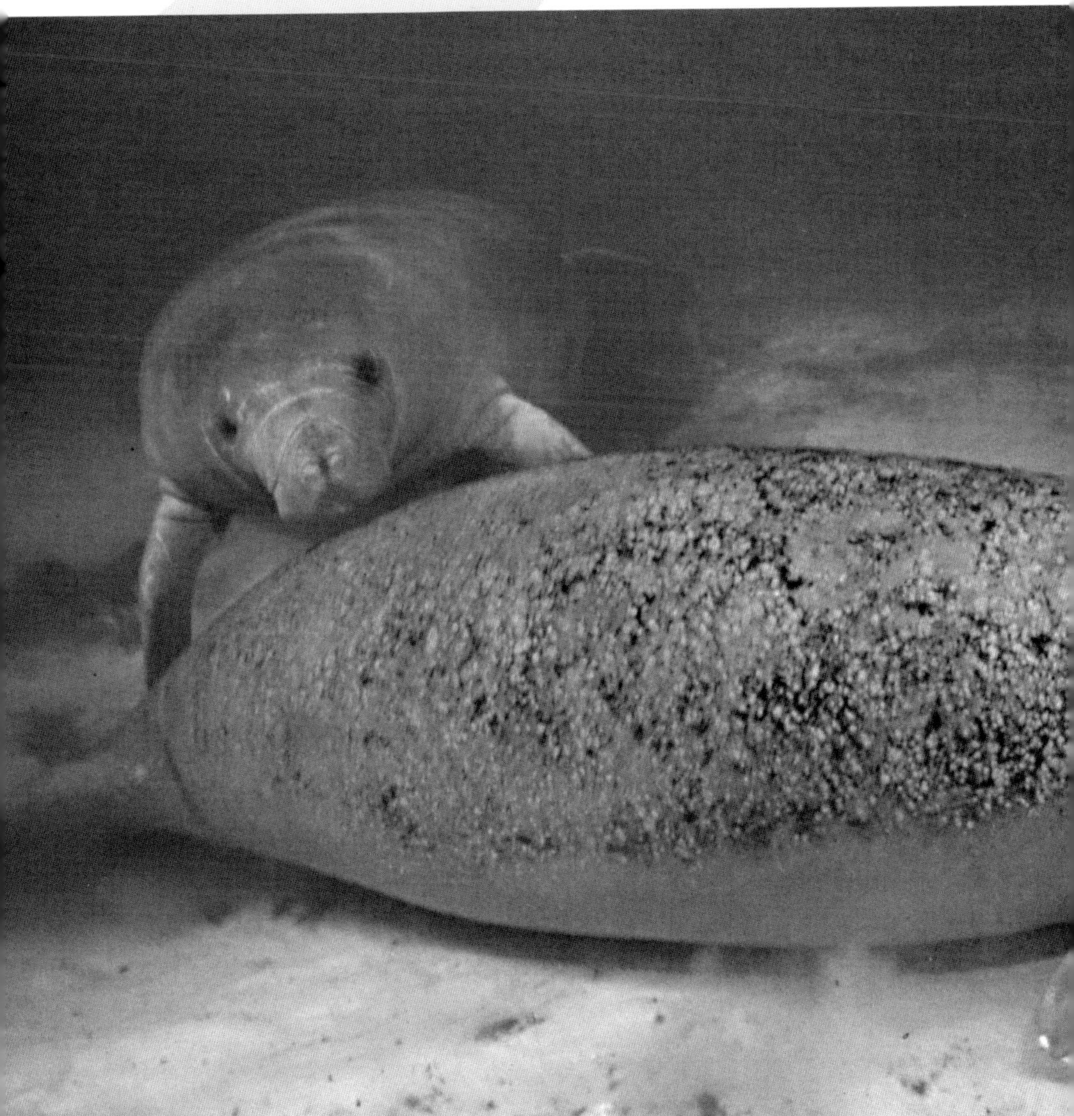

Unfortunately, some things floating on the water shouldn't be there. These include soda and beer cans, plastic bags, six-pack holders, and other litter.

Manatees are very curious. This often gets them into trouble. Ropes or tires can be deadly. Manatees can become tangled in ropes or caught in tires. They might not be able to surface to breathe. Then they would die.

Dudley grew. His color changed from dark to light gray.

His skin was very wrinkled. The outside layer was always peeling off. It was like a person's skin that has been sunburned. If it hadn't peeled, algae would have covered Dudley's body.

All the manatees that live near Florida are West Indian manatees. There are three other types of manatees.

The West African manatees live in waters off the coast of West Africa. Not much is known about them.

The Amazonian manatee has smooth skin. It lives only in the fresh, shallow waters of the Amazon and Orinoco Rivers.

It's the smallest of the manatees. It has no nails on its flippers. Florida manatees do. They have three or four at the tips of their flippers.

The dugong is a family member. It has smooth skin. It doesn't have nails. And its tail is notched instead of rounded. The male has tusks.

Dugongs live in the coastal waters of the Indian and Pacific Oceans. They are hunted for food.

Another type of manatee was Steller's sea cow. It is extinct. It was the only group member that lived in cold water.

It had dark, rough skin. Its tail was forked. It didn't have teeth. It's believed that it fed entirely on algae.

The sea cow was the largest. It grew over 30 feet long. And it weighed up to 7,000 pounds.

In 1741, these sea cows were discovered in the Arctic waters of the Bering Strait. They were killed for food by whalers. Hunters killed them for fur. In less than 30 years, they were extinct.

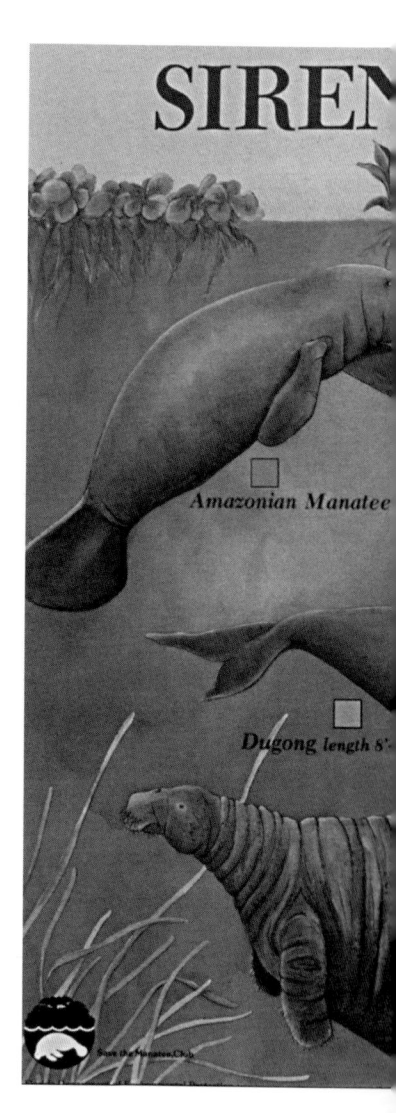

All manatees belong to the order of Sirenians. The water mammals within this order eat nothing but plants. All other water mammals eat meat too.

Manatees spend six to eight hours a day eating. They eat 10 percent of their body weight. That could be as much as 150 pounds a day. The intestine of an adult is about 130 feet long.

"Save the Manatee" poster, photo by Jeff Foott

Dudley was related to the elephant and the hyrax. The hyrax is a small, furry animal that looks like a rodent. The manatee, the elephant, and the hyrax all have the same ancestors.

Manatees and elephants are alike in many ways. They both have the same kind of thick skin and thin hair. They have the same kind of digestive tract.

They both have eyes that seem too small for the rest of their bodies. They both have nails. And their teeth are similar.

Scientists believe that manatees were once land animals. They ate plants and waded along riverbanks and shorelines.

But about 50 million years ago, a change took place. It took many, many years. But finally, the manatees' hind legs disappeared. Their front legs became flippers.

They left the land to become water animals. But they continued breathing air and living on plants.

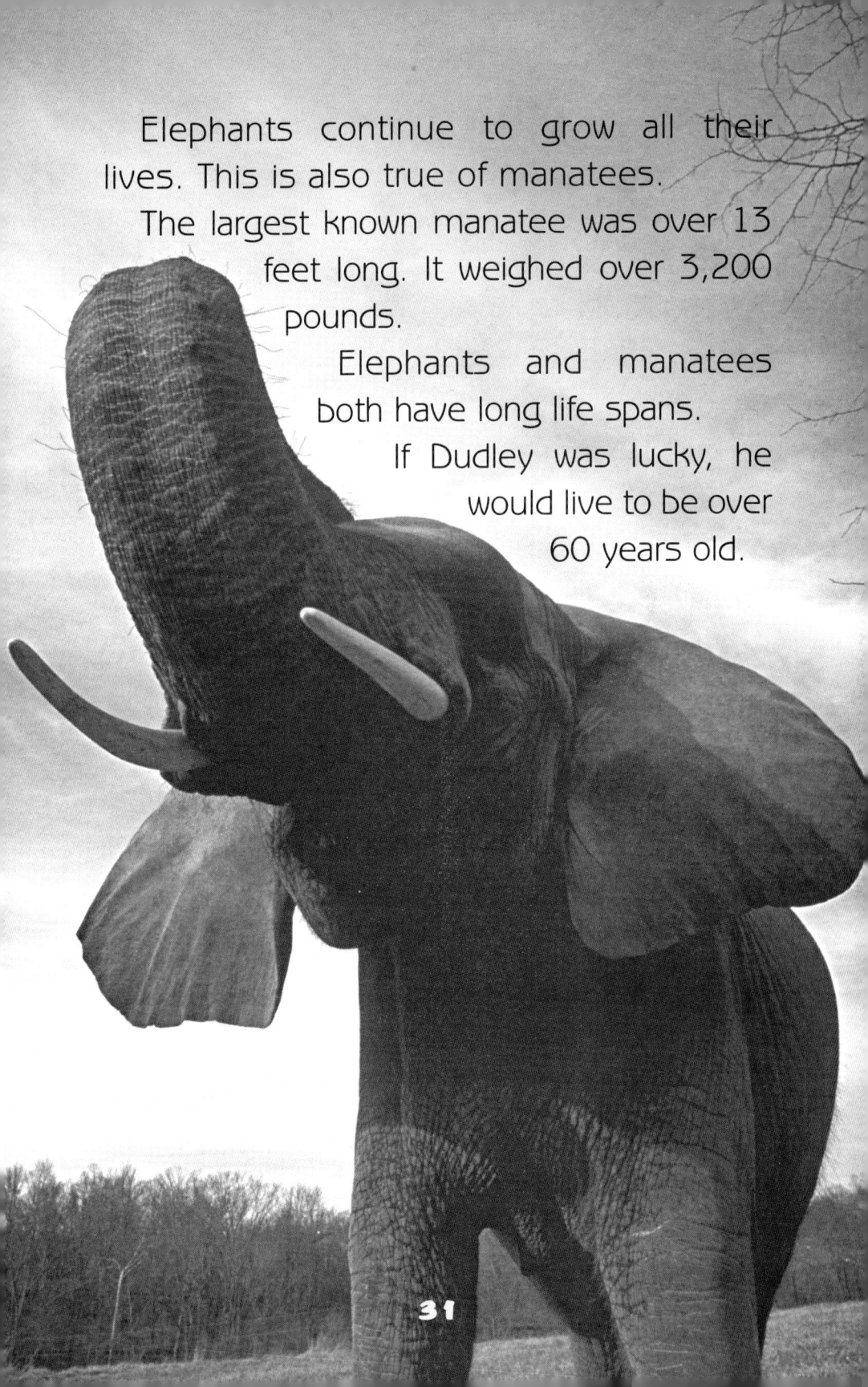

Elephants continue to grow all their lives. This is also true of manatees.

The largest known manatee was over 13 feet long. It weighed over 3,200 pounds.

Elephants and manatees both have long life spans. If Dudley was lucky, he would live to be over 60 years old.

chapter 4

Dudley was two months old. He weighed 125 pounds.

It was midsummer. And it was very hot in Florida.

There were many boats on the water. Dudley didn't like the sound of the motors. It was scary.

Strange things were moving underwater too. He didn't know what they were.

He didn't know about divers yet. He only knew that they were something to stay away from. Some tried to get close to him and his mother.

Once Dudley saw a diver trying to ride a manatee. It squealed and tried to get away.

Many people think that manatees were brought to Florida from other places. Some think manatees were brought in to eat water plants. These plants clog the waterways.

But manatees are Florida natives. And studies show that there aren't enough manatees to eat the plants. There are only about 2,600 alive today.

There is proof that manatees have been in Florida waters for a long time. Fossils have been found. These date back at least 45 million years.

Early American Indians hunted the manatee for food. They used the hides for shoes and other clothing.

Then Spanish colonists hunted and killed the large sea mammals. They wanted the meat, leather, and oil.

In 1893, hunting manatees was banned. But the population has been slow to grow.

Manatees are now protected by a 1972 United States law. A 1978 Florida law also protects them.

It is against the law to harm, bother, trap, or kill manatees. People can be fined. They can even be put in jail for breaking the law. But still many don't pay attention to the laws.

35

Many boats were on the water. So Dudley and his mother spent a lot of time resting on the river bottom.

Dudley liked resting there. Sometimes he turned on his back. He watched turtles and fish swim by.

He would often bump a turtle with his nose. The turtle would move away. It went as fast as it could. Dudley thought this was fun.

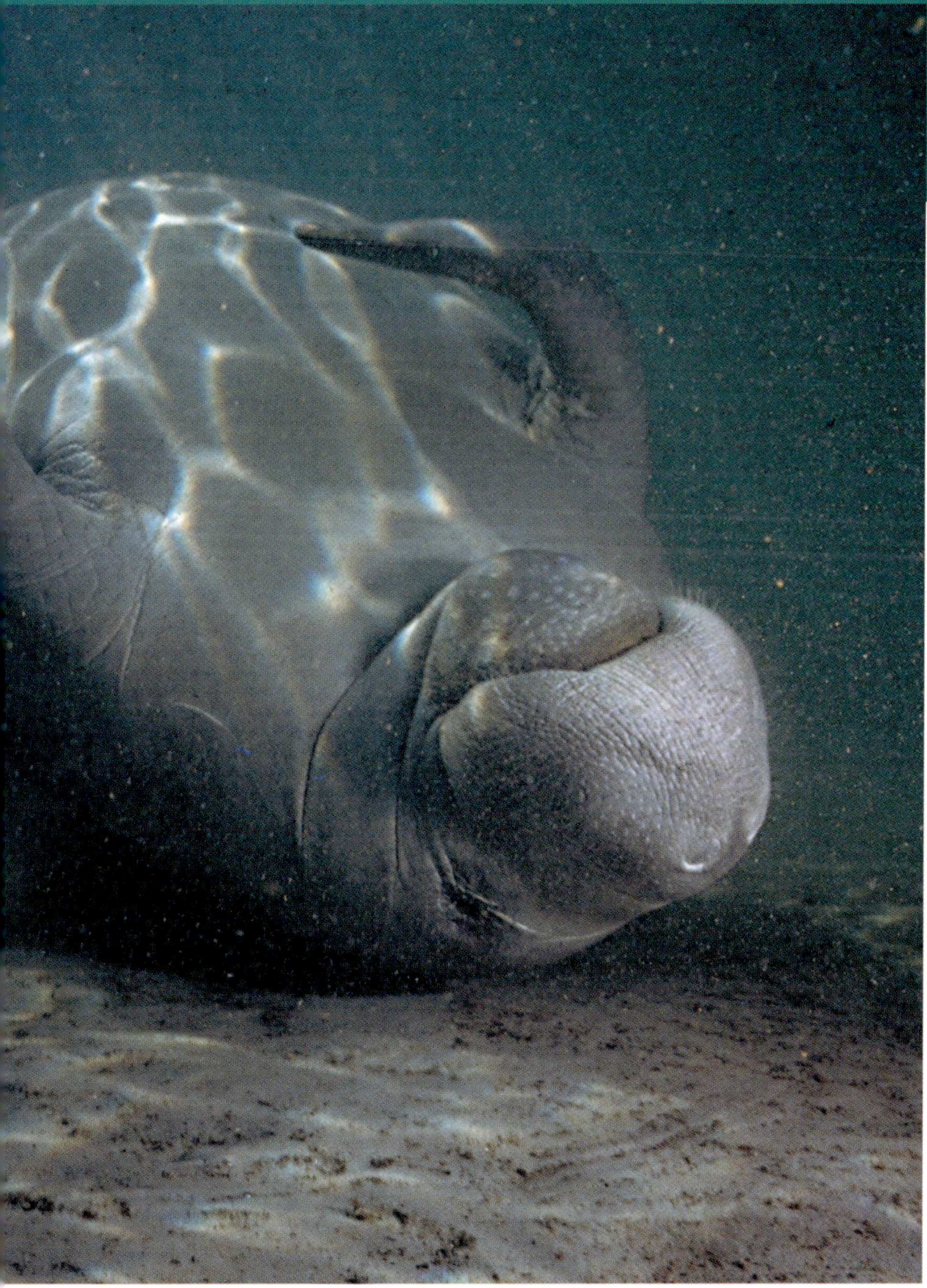

Once in a while, a river otter would slide down the riverbank. It would splash into the water.

Dudley's life was never dull. All of the other manatees and wildlife nearby kept him company.

He saw beavers, squirrels, and whales. Other wildlife included dolphins, alligators, ducks, eagles, and water turkeys.

People come from all over to see the rare manatee and other wildlife.

chapter 5

One day, there was a bad accident. It was close to where Dudley and his mother were feeding.

A young female was hurt. She had been crushed against the river bottom by a barge.

Her loud squeals frightened Dudley. He swam close to his mother. He pushed his nose against her. He made squeaking sounds.

In a short time, help arrived. The young cow was taken to a place where hurt manatees are cared for.

There are several places like this in Florida. Doctors treat the animals. Other people feed and care for them until they can be released.

In 1969, a young male manatee was trapped in a storm drain. He was almost dead when he was found. Rescuers took him to a refuge.

He spent two years there. The workers named him Sewer Sam.

When he was well and strong, he was returned to the open waters. He was the first manatee to be treated and later released.

Many can't be released. Their injuries are too bad. They can't survive on their own.

Some manatees have spent many years in captivity. Rosie is a manatee that has been in captivity since 1968.

A pair of manatees, Romeo and Juliet, were at the Miami Seaquarium for a long time. They had mated several times. But Juliet never had a calf.

Doctors thought it might be because of diet. The manatees ate mostly lettuce and cabbage.

Minerals were added. They were also fed carrots, apples, and bananas.

In time, Juliet gave birth to a healthy calf. The female calf was named Lorelei.

It was the first time a pair of manatees had mated and produced a calf in captivity. Juliet had been a foster mother to other calves though.

By using this diet for all the manatees, more calves have been born in captivity.

Amanda, a cow, was rescued after being badly injured by a motorboat propeller. Her two-week-old baby was rescued with her. It was on December 25, 1973. The baby was named Ariel.

Amanda still lives in captivity. And she has given birth to more calves—Betsy and Star.

When Ariel was eight years old, she had a male calf. It was born very early one morning. So it was named Sunrise.

If something happened to Dudley's mother, he would probably die. Calves depend on their mothers for up to two years. Even after they begin eating plants, they still need their mother's milk.

By late summer, Dudley had begun to eat water plants. He liked all the good things that grew in the water.

Dudley and his mother moved several times during the summer. They moved to new feeding grounds.

Sometimes they grazed in freshwater. Sometimes they grazed in water that was part fresh and part salty. But they always stayed where the water was shallow.

Dudley was munching on a juicy plant. He pushed the plant into his mouth with a flipper. Then he cleaned his teeth with his flipper. Pieces of food were stuck between them.

Suddenly, there was a loud roar.

Something was zooming toward him. He moved out of the way as fast as he could.

A small motorboat appeared. It was going very fast. And it just missed Dudley.

He looked around for his mother. Where was she?

Dudley couldn't see her anywhere. He began to squeal. His squeals grew louder and louder.

Dudley had never been separated from his mother before. He was so scared. He continued squealing.

After a long time, he heard an answering squeal. It was his mother. He knew it was. But where was she?

It was several more minutes before he saw her. She was swimming toward him. She was crying loudly.

The cow had a cut on her body. It was bleeding. Luckily, it wasn't deep. She had tried to get out of the way of the boat. But she was struck by a propeller.

Dudley and his mother put their faces together. They kissed and nuzzled, making soft cooing sounds.

They were both safe, for now.

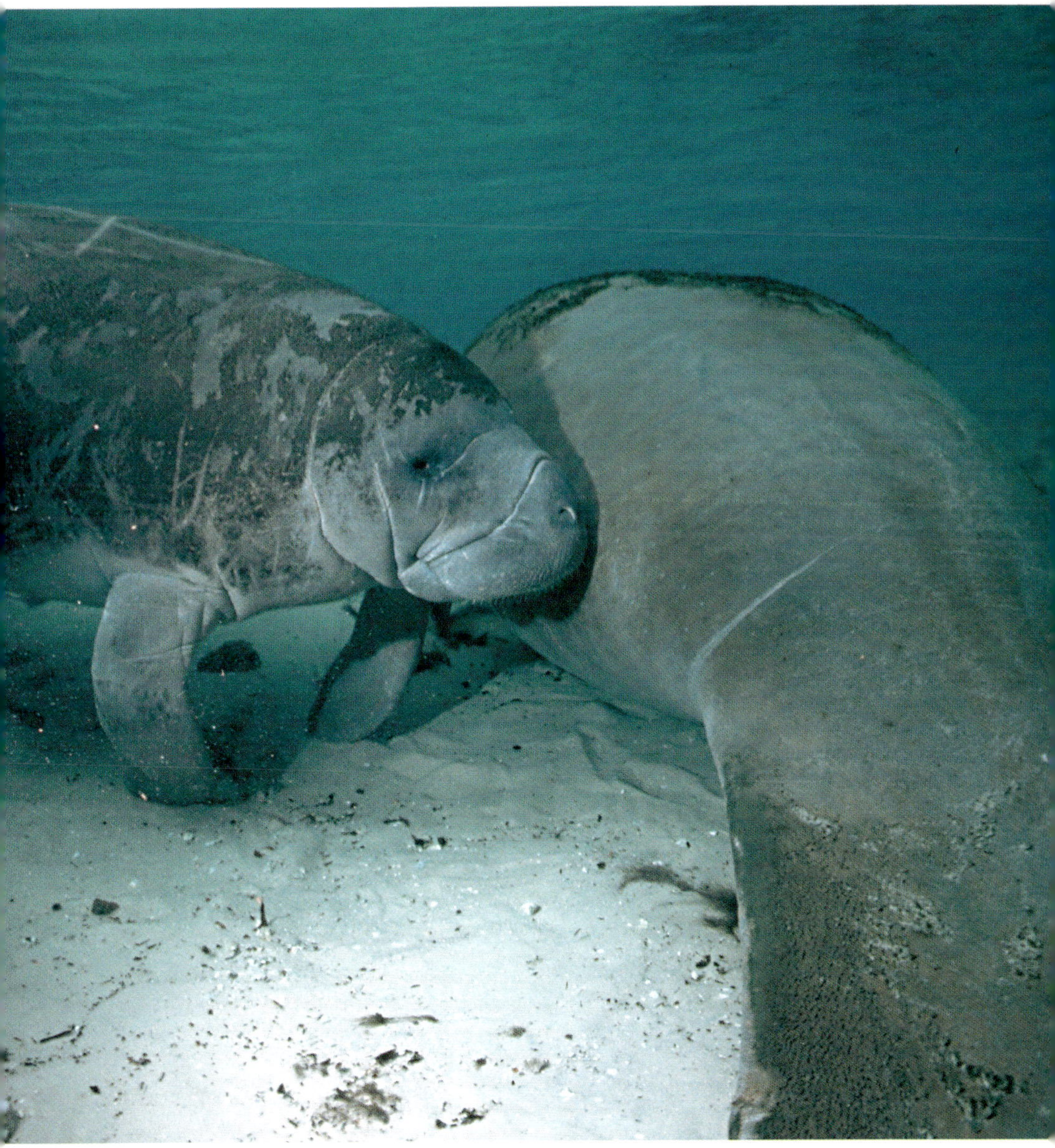

chapter 6

By the end of October, Dudley weighed 300 pounds.

When he was a year old, he could weigh 800 pounds. And he could be over six feet long.

Dudley probably wouldn't breed until he was eight years old. He might be even older.

Females breed when they are about five or six years old. They have a calf every two or three years. The male has no part in raising the calf.

In the summer, Dudley and his mother fed in many different places. They found places with plenty of food. And they found places where they felt safe.

But now the waters were getting cooler. When water temperatures dropped below 70 degrees, Dudley and the other manatees moved to warmer places.

Florida tourists are able to see more manatees in the winter than in summer.

In the summer months, a few manatees can be found in places as far west as Louisiana. They travel as far north as the Carolinas and Virginia. Some can even be found in the waters of Central and South America.

But in the winter months, manatees form herds. As many as 200 can be found in places where the water is warm.

More than 300 manatees were seen at one power and light company. Water released by the plant was very warm. Other industrial sites also release warm water that attracts manatees.

Some manatees find natural springs with warm water.

If manatees can't find warm water, they may not survive. Waters below 68 degrees can carry diseases that kill them.

Dudley and his mother reached the warm water in plenty of time. It was also a good place to feed. Dudley's mother had been coming back to the same place since she was born. For her first three years, she had been with her mother.

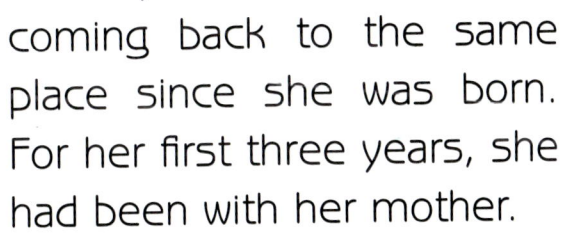

Now she was on her own. And she had her own calf. But she remembered everything her mother had taught her. Now she would share what she had learned.

She would show Dudley the best routes to travel. She would teach him where to find winter shelters and feeding places.

She would teach him to stay underwater as much as possible when motorboats were near.

Every day, more manatees came from other places. There were nearly a hundred in the winter group with Dudley and his mother.

During the winter, there would be warm days. Then the manatees would move to other warm water spots. But it would be March or April before they left their wintering grounds.

It has been said that a manatee has a face that only a mother could love. Yet, sailors of long ago thought manatees were mermaids. No one knows exactly why.

Christopher Columbus referred to them as mermaids. He wrote, "They are not as beautiful as they are painted. But to some extent they have a human appearance in the face."

53

Many writers have mentioned manatees in stories. In *A Midsummer Night's Dream*, Shakespeare called them "sea-maids." And Jules Verne wrote of them in *The Mysterious Island*.

Hopefully future writers won't have to refer to manatees as extinct or animals of the past.

For more information about manatees, contact

Save the Manatee Club
500 N. Maitland Ave.
Maitland, FL 32751
(800) 432-5646

www.savethemanatee.org

"Save the Manatee" is a registered trademark of Save the Manatee Club, Inc., a nonprofit 501 (c) (3) organization, registered in the state of Florida.